MEASURING MASTERS

Measuring Temperature

by Martha E. H. Rustad

PEBBLE
a capstone imprint

Pebble Plus is published by Pebble
1710 Roe Crest Drive, North Mankato,
Minnesota 56003
www.mycapstone.com

Library of Congress Cataloging-in-Publication Data
Library of Congress Cataloging-in-Publication data is available on the Library of Congress website.
ISBN 978-1-9771-0369-7 (library binding)
ISBN 978-1-9771-0554-7 (paperback)
ISBN 978-1-9771-0376-5 (eBook PDF)

Editorial Credits
Michelle Parkin, editor; Elyse White, designer; Heather Mauldin, media researcher;
Laura Manthe, production specialist

Photo Credits
iStockphoto: andresr, 5, FatCamera, 21, M00Nkey, 19, Paul Bradbury, 15; Shutterstock: A3pfamily, 11, Africa Studio,
13, Andrey_Popov, 9, BlueOrange Studio, cover, Lopolo, 7, makuromi, 17

Design Elements
Shutterstock: blue_bubble, interior, DarkPlatypus, cover

Note to Parents and Teachers

The Measuring Masters set supports national curriculum standards for mathematical practice
related to measurement and data. This book describes and illustrates how to measure temperature.
The images support early readers in understanding the text. The repetition of words and phrases
helps early readers learn new words. This book also introduces early readers to subject-specific
vocabulary words, which are defined in the Glossary section. Early readers may need assistance
to read some words and to use the Table of Contents, Glossary, Read More, Internet Sites, Critical
Thinking Questions, and Index sections of the book.

Printed and bound in China.
970

Table of Contents

Hot or Cold?

I want to play outside today.

But I don't know what to wear.

Is the weather hot or cold outside?

We need to find out the temperature.

Measuring Tools

Temperature measures how hot or cold something is. A low temperature means something is cold. When something is hot, it has a high temperature.

Thermometers measure temperature.
Some thermometers show
the temperature in
degrees Fahrenheit (°F).
Others show temperatures
in degrees Celsius (°C).
Some thermometers show both.

Some thermometers are made of glass.

The liquid inside goes up and down to show the temperature.

There are also digital thermometers.

The temperature appears on the screen.

Some thermometers are
used for cooking.
Dad checks the turkey's temperature
to see if it's safe to eat.
He cooked it just right. Dinner time!

Temperature Examples

I feel sick.

Mom uses a thermometer

to check my temperature.

My temperature is 101.2°F (38.4°C).

I have a fever.

The oven has a thermometer.

We read it to see when

the oven is hot.

We bake muffins at 350°F (177°C).

An outside thermometer tells

us the air temperature.

The temperature is cold in winter.

In summer the temperature is warm.

Let's play outside.

Do I need a hat and gloves?

Or can I wear shorts?

It is 83°F (28°C).

I can wear shorts!

Glossary

Celsius (SEL-see-uhs)—a scale for measuring temperature in degrees; water freezes at 0 degrees Celsius

Fahrenheit (FAYR-uhn-hyt)—a scale for measuring temperature in degrees; water freezes at 32 degrees Fahrenheit

fever (FEE-vehr)—a rise in body temperature; a fever can mean that you are sick

thermometer (thur-MOM-uh-tur)—a tool that measures temperature

Read More

Bernhardt, Carolyn. *Temperature.* Blastoff Readers: Science Starters. Minneapolis: Bellwether Media, 2019.

Polinsky, Paige V. *Super Simple Experiments with Heat and Cold: Fun and Innovative Science Projects.* Super Simple Science at Work. Minneapolis: Abdo, 2017.

Roberts, Abigail B. *Using a Thermometer.* Super Science Tools. New York: Gareth Stevens, 2018.

Internet Sites

Use FactHound to find Internet sites related to this book.

Visit *www.facthound.com*

Just type in 9781977103697 and go.

Super-cool stuff!

Check out projects, games and lots more at
www.capstonekids.com

Critical Thinking Questions

1. The temperature is 32°F. What should you put on before you play outside?

2. What is the temperature outside today? What do you think the temperature will be like six months from today?

3. Your temperature reads 98.6°F. Do you have a fever? Why or why not?

Index